Wonderment

Also by Brenda Eldridge and published by Ginninderra Press

Poetry
The Silver Cord
It's All Good
A Personal View
Facing Cancer
From My Garden
Best Heard & Seen
Scarves
Tangled Roots: new & selected poems
Elemental (Pocket Poets)
Forgotten Dreams (Pocket Poets)

Non-fiction
Down by the River
Tales From My Patagonia
It's Still Out There
There's a Rainbow Serpent In My Garden
Eastwards
From Patagonia to Australia
Forty Green (Pocket Places)

Edited by Brenda Eldridge and published by Ginninderra Press

Brave Enough To Be a Poet
The Heart of Port Adelaide
Collecting Writers

Brenda Eldridge

Wonderment

Dedicated with heartfelt thanks to

my beloved Stephen, who makes living in a world of
gentleness and joy possible

Annette, who is brave enough to travel with me

my several families for their unswerving support

You all fill my life with love

Wonderment
ISBN 978 1 76041 018 6
Copyright © Brenda Eldridge 2015
Cover photograph and design by Brenda Eldridge

First published 2015 by
GINNINDERRA PRESS
PO Box 3461 Port Adelaide 5015 Australia
www.ginninderrapress.com.au

Contents

Watching the Watcher	7
The Mountains of Semaphore	8
Flowing Like Honey	9
Brief Applause	10
Little Boats	11
Dream Garden	12
More the Merrier	13
Musing	14
Valiant Heart	15
Leaping For Joy	16
A Different Pleasure Dome	17
Pelican Pace	18
Blippy Fish	19
Nothing new about autumn leaves	20
In the Wild	21
Gardening Surprises	22
Moonlit	23
Closing of a Day	24
Spinning Tops	25
Untouchables	26
Swimming With a Seal	27
Mermaid Hair	28
Reluctant	29
Blue Boat	30
Misquoting	31
Caves of Colour and Light	32
Passion	33
Contrasts	34
Reasons to Smile	35
First Day of Winter	36

Wonderland	37
Afterglow	38
Melted Cheese	39
Between Heaven and Earth	40
Layer Upon Layer	41
Mariners	42
Comforting Sounds	43
Clean Sweep	44
All Wrapped Up	45
Moving	46
Big Breakfast	47
Ah Well	48
Endless Questions	49
Promises of Spring	50
Pastoral	51
Bush Walk	52
Denial	53
Garden Drama	54
It's Still Out There	55
Red Wattlebird	56
Petunias and Pansies	57
Patience	58
Crow's Nest	59
Fairies at Work	60
Hot Stuff	61
Flower Power	62
Slowing Heart and Mind	63

Watching the Watcher

Before the sun was quite up
I sat on the rocks beside the tidal reach
and gave thanks again
for the good fortune that brought me here
more interesting by far than being beside the sea
for all that I had seals for company yesterday
as I paddled in the chill of late autumn

Here I witness the ebb and flow of the tides
watch in awe as dolphins cruise   leap   dive
I smile with quiet glee to see
egrets   cormorants   gulls
all in search of breakfast

And as the sun gleams off the windows opposite
like two eyes watching me watching,
the still waters undulate gently
as two pelicans paddle through the
brilliant gold smudge of reflected sunlight
becoming even more mysterious beings

While all around
the flutter of wings   birds calling

And barely visible in the pale blue sky
a tiny sickle moon watches me watching

The Mountains of Semaphore

I cannot make claim to this piece of whimsy
but I can write of it all the same

Strong winds overnight took out the power

We sat in the gloom eating our breakfast
glad to have a gas stove

A saucepan of water was boiled to make coffee
and another used for making porridge –
it took me back years

We watched the tidal reach – usually so still –
a mass of little white-capped waves
leaping as if to get over the banks   to no avail –
it needs the help of a king tide

In the western sky
the full moon delicately sank behind
a bank of billowing heavy rain clouds

Then suddenly the sun must have climbed high
because the same clouds became rimmed
with pink-tinged cream

And as Stephen said
'There's snow on the mountains of Semaphore'

Flowing Like Honey

We sit under the veranda
to enjoy our morning coffee
and I am aware of different sounds

In the distance magpies and crows

Within the walled garden
the constant chatter of sparrows
soft exchanges of the pigeons

Wind gently passing through
the dried leaves of the Japanese maple
making them whisper a magical song
before they fall sighing to the ground

Meanwhile the wind chimes sing –
not tinkling with gaiety
like the ones upstairs
these are long metal tubes
that are mellifluous
which means
flowing like honey

Brief Applause

There was nothing unusual
about the cormorant
taking off from the still water

What caught my attention
was a single slap
from a wing or foot
that reminded me of
someone at a concert
listening to an unknown piece of music
and thinking it had ended
began to applaud
one loud solitary clap
only to find there were
two more notes to be played…

I feel like applauding the cormorants
each time they take off…
it seems to require such effort
to get airborne

Little Boats

A row of six or seven
small dinghies and wooden boats
were tethered to the jetty

I loved their individuality
painted pink   blue   white

A length of thick rope around each rim
protected them from bumping
into each other or something else

I wondered about the bite
out of the back of each of them
then worked out it was where
an outboard motor would sit

I guess I was still thinking
in terms of oars
and rowboats
long ago
messing about on a river…

Dream Garden

Unusual for me I woke remembering a dream:

Beneath towering trees
were tranquil green-tinged goldfish ponds
one leading to another
linked by singing sparkling waterfalls
each edged with large lichen-covered boulders

Lilies floated serenely
amidst their dinner plate leaves
ferns added lushness
like lace to a ballgown

In the far corner a garden shed
and hanging from a wall
a wooden box like the ones used
to take fruit to market
filled with sandstone-coloured pebbles

In the hollowed-out centre
like nestling eggs
three larger-than-life pears
tinged with red – perfect for eating

Off to the side
a narrow straight path beckoned –
it was lined with dainty trees
black-timbered from the rain
their leaves coloured pale lemon
a weak sun making them seem almost transparent
many plastered to the ground
slick and slippery for the unwary

More the Merrier

One dolphin gliding through the water
lifts my heart   lightens my mind
I find myself smiling for no reason
except the sheer joy
of seeing such a glorious creature

This morning there are five!
Mother and baby and escorts
swooshing and leaping
slapping tails on the surface
and even I can see
the shoal of small fish
close to the bank
that is providing them with late breakfast

I don't bother trying to measure
if my pleasure is five times greater –
enough to be glad and feel the smile
stretching ever wider
and become a chuckle of delight

Musing

We have learned to recognise
the sound of the plane
that circles and climbs overhead

We know when the pilot cuts his engine
moments later the parachutists
will come into view
yellow   blue   red
usually four of them

Sometimes eerily they appear
from the misty clouds
drifting down like giant dandelion-clock seed heads
and I wonder what exotic flowers
would bloom from these
if they took hold in the land
they so gently fall upon

Valiant Heart

We don't know much about dolphins
I simply love to watch them
any time of day or night
as they frequent our part of the tidal reach

They are the epitome of sensuousness
whether sparkling and flashing in sunlight
or gleaming in moonlight

The baby is still learning about buoyancy
not so much grace as a
heave up and a sinking down

But he has a valiant heart
and bravely keeps up with his family

Leaping For Joy

From the beginning
the baby dolphin has swum
beside his mum
with perfectly synchronised movements
heaving his little body through the water
while other members of the pod
kept an ever-watchful guard

As the little one has grown
all have worked together
a lethal hunting pack
even in the quiet of the tidal reach

Today the baby struck off alone
he leapt again and again
clear out of the water
turning over mid-flight
to land on his back

I'm not sure how efficient he was
at catching fish
but he was having such fun
leaping for joy
and our delight watching him
knew no bounds

A Different Pleasure Dome

In the middle of the night
when all was still and quiet
the half moon shone serenely
in her bed among the clouds
that billowed like a luxurious
silvery down-filled quilt

Intrigued by the brightness
I wandered into my studio
to look out of the window
to the garden below

The prostrate rosemary bush
with its mass of pale mauve flowers
looking like snow in the moonlight
had become a mysterious scented dome
and I went back to bed
falling asleep half-smiling
wondering what it would be like
to live under a rosemary bush

Perhaps not so different from how I live now
travelling light   like a snail
with my home on my back

Not quite the pleasure dome
of Kubla Khan in Xanadu

Pelican Pace

No smooth gliding like the swans
with their regal grace
as if they need to make no effort
to propel themselves through the water

The pelican came close
and gently chugged along
leaving a wake curling wide
like the soft folds
of a satin ballgown
mid-dance under a sunlit chandelier

Blippy Fish

Sometimes when it is dark and still
you can see countless little circle ripples
breaking the smooth surface
of the tidal reach

And there is a sound
like a handful of gravel
thrown into the water
only with the volume turned down
so it is more like a hiss

It is the blippy fish
who only come at night

Nothing new about autumn leaves

The leaves on the plane trees
are mostly still green
just a few with brown dried edges

They dance in the sun and wind
and I can hear them singing
'Let us free   Let us fly'

Further along the path
are piles of crunchy leaves
huddled up against the wall

How could I resist?

For a few moments
I was a child again
kicking up autumn leaves
glorying in the rustling sounds
remembering copper beeches
oaks   chestnuts
Oh! and conkers
a hidden treasure
amongst the dross

In the Wild

Our neighbour's palm tree
afforded us such pleasure
when the giant seed pod exploded
into a mass of shining gold

Word went around among the rainbow lorikeets
more than a dozen flocked in
dazzling us with their brilliant colours
their dexterity as they hung upside down
and every which way to feast –
all the time noisily squawking
with such exuberance

Who cares for table manners
when gourmet delight is on offer?

Now the palm tree offers us a new event

Among the leafy fronds
the faded and empty seed pods
a long spike with a short tassel at the tip
is reaching up
reminding me of a giraffe's tail
or even a tawny lion
stealthily creeping through the veldt…

Gardening Surprises

In the spring
I planted peas in the vegetable patch
so we could enjoy them freshly picked
and among the plants a beautiful
deep purple sweet-pea flower appeared
smelling as lovely as any I have known

I carefully hoarded the seeds
in a blank envelope
putting them in the cupboard
with other similar envelopes
waiting for autumn
before putting them in the planter pots
at the base of the wooden garden arch

When I came to do this
I made an attempt to economise
by topping up the soil in the pots
with some from the garden

To my surprise instead of sweet peas
I thought I had tomato plants
perhaps from a stray
that had dropped to the ground
during the summer –
but patience they say is its own reward
and I have coriander growing
among the french marigolds

I do wonder where the sweet peas went
and will they appear among
the next crop of broad beans or…

Moonlit

The night was warm velvet
the tidal reach black and still

Dolphins made the waters move
in swaths of silver sensuousness

A lone pelican became an unusual shape
as it went midnight fishing
only visible as the moon lit up
white feathers and long pale beak

Closing of a Day

Carried on the warm night air
across the still tidal reach
music from a nearby outdoor concert

The deep throb of drums and bass
a soaring voice
haunting   unearthly

Silently a lone canoeist
paddled past
leaving a rippling wake

For a moment he was joined
by the graceful sweep
of a dolphin's fin

They were silhouetted against the reflection
of a silver and apricot sky
ornamented by wispy grey clouds
highlighted in deep pink

The closing of a day

Spinning Tops

We wandered mesmerised
through the acres of a native garden
such extraordinary blooms
so very different
to the standard garden varieties

One rather tatty-looking small tree
with its silver-grey leaves
didn't have the usual gum nuts

These were like a child's spinning top
complete with a handle
and a point to place on a smooth surface

Oh how my fingers itched
to pluck them and take them home
but as always
the natural world is best left

And I chafe at having to be sensible

Untouchables

I cycle along a street
lined with big native lilac trees

Perfume from their blossoms
fills the air
along with the sound of birdsong

I can touch neither with my hands
yet they both fill my senses

Swimming With a Seal

The sea was silver-blue
gently swelling to the shore
early morning cool
embracing me like silk
I floated utterly at peace

I walked out onto the beach
turned to look at the water
and there
only a few metres away
from where I had been
a seal doing as I had done
just lazily luxuriating

One moment its flipper was raised
the next its tail high
then it lay on its back
as if soaking up the sun

How could I do anything
but laugh out loud with joy
and of course
hastily take out the camera

The gods were kind
I have a picture to remind me
of those magical moments
swimming with a seal

Mermaid Hair

The sea was exquisite to play in –
rough and tumbly
with patches of warm and cool –
so good to go under the waves
moving through the water
hair floating back and forth
with the jerky motion
of my swimming strokes

I cycled home
glad of my cardigan
because the wind had cold fingers
where my clothes were wet

I gladly stripped off
to have a hot shower
when I noticed mermaid hair
on the bathroom floor

Stephen wasn't taken in with that idea
so reluctantly I took out the vacuum cleaner
to suck up the broken strands of seaweed

But we both remembered him
drawing mermaids in the sand
for his little granddaughter
and she used seaweed
for mermaid hair

Reluctant

The baby seal was content
to bask on the warm dry sand

Mum had other ideas
and gently but determinedly
encouraged the little chap
to go down to the water's edge

There she started having a chat
with another Mum
and probably hoped the babies
would play together

But not her baby

He galloped bleating
back up the beach
and no amount of calling
would make him change his mind

Blue Boat

Moored to the old jetty
at American River on Kangaroo Island
a blue rowboat bobbed gently

In the stillness of morning
I could see evidence of the loving hand
that had painted the inside
a darker shade than the outside

And I not liking to go on boats much
felt some mysterious call
a beckoning
and for a moment
I wanted to clamber on board
pick up the oars as I did as a child
when my dad hired a boat
to take us out on a backwater
of the river Thames –
all tranquil overhanging trees
green water   white swans…

So different yet somehow the same

Misquoting

I deliberately misquote
because it is easier to remember:
a loaf of bread   a flask of wine
a book of verse   and thou beside me
in the wilderness…

We sat in the balmy afternoon sun
grazing on a platter of Mediteranean-style food:
goat's cheese   roasted eggplant
sun-dried tomatoes   black olives
grilled chorizo   ciabatta bread
and sipping sparkling wine

There were soft voices in the background
and tiny brown wrens
behaving like sparrows looking for crumbs

Below us the hills folded neatly
and trees filled the triangle
that led down to a combe

Clouds rendered the sea silvery blue
while large ships passed smoothly silently by
and across Backstairs Passage the mainland slept
brown and dried-out after a long summer

No not the Rubaiyat – more Epicurus
the way we love to be together
good wine   good food
good company   good conversation…

Yes another misquote

Caves of Colour and Light

In the late afternoon
the trees were breathtaking

We drove through enchanted tunnels
of trunks and branches
a mixture of
grey   cream   brown
and foliage
dark green   blue-green   evergreen
that opened up into caves of colour

Leaves of pale green turning to lemon
fading to become golden pennies

Orange   scarlet   crimson leaves
like open hands   shivering

The sun sent shafts of light among them all
and some became sparks of silver

But for all the vibrant hues
there remained a delicacy
a shimmering of colour and light

Passion

Across this secluded valley
luxuriant vivid green vines
hug the gentle contours of the earth
surrounded by blue-grey-clad eucalypts
creating an unexpected harmony

The sultry evening sun hides among
heavily laden inky-coloured clouds –
a storm is building while tiny finches
the size of gum leaves
dart from tree to tree

Single raindrops ping loudly
on the perspex veranda roof –
suddenly there is a torrent of water –
streaks of silver obscuring the view
turning all to shades of grey

Green-cream slender branches toss in the wind
lightning flashes golden in the gloom
thunder cracks overhead and rumbles away
the roar of the rain drowns all other sounds

And miraculously all is still and quiet –
birds sing an ecstatic chorus
water drips in runnels off the roof
heat lingers in the air

Lightning flickers on and on
into the darkness of night

Contrasts

Coming out of the warm bathroom
after the luxury of a hot shower
I stepped out onto the balcony
into another world

I wrapped an alpaca serape around my shoulders
but still I shivered in the cold air

The tidal reach reflected perfectly
puffy grey-blue clouds   a pale pink sky
night slipping away to make room for the day

A pelican flew past so low
its wingtips almost touched the surface –
he too was mirror-imaged

Tiny ripples appeared   gone in a moment –
mystery creatures calling this home

Gulls began harassing a cormorant
intent on diving for breakfast

A man walked upside down beneath the bridge

Grey clouds in the west
were backlit by rosy-golden hues

The eastern sky shrouded in heavy cloud
too dense for the glowing colours of dawn

I am wonder-filled to witness
this world of contrasts

Reasons to Smile

The winter sun was barely warm on my face
my legs were cold from paddling in the sea
but the jetty's wooden pylons
shone like lustrous silver

Bright white-capped waves rolled laughing to shore
gurgling over the sand

A cormorant teased – visible one second
gone the next

A dog was running hither and yon
barking as it chased gulls
who kept just out of reach

There was a lightness in the air

It felt like everyone was simply having fun

First Day of Winter

The watery yellow sun
was sliding all too quickly
down behind a bank of cloud
hemming with gold
wide smooth ripples
made by a passing and hidden dolphin
in the otherwise still tidal reach

With one last gasp of wonder
the sun was gone

Great shafts of hazy light
fanned out into the heavens
fading to paint grey clouds
briefly with pink and gold
that was reflected on the water

A tender passing into this new season

Wonderland

Snowy white they danced on the air
sun gleaming on their wings

Waves ran like mythical horses
prancing in the surf
sending up spray
feet gliding over the seaweed
as it tried to hold them tethered

Behind them all a storm was coming

Clouds dark grey and heavy with rain
making ethereal this wonderland
Of wind   sun   sea   silver gulls

Afterglow

This afterglow takes my breath away
and my mind fumbles for words
to match the colours changing
too quickly to name

Lemon turning moment by moment
to warm apricot with a hint of pink

The world is turning
of this there can be no doubt

I watch this great halo of brightness
sinking lower   narrowing   deepening   mellowing

Hazy blue of night like a persistent weight
pressing   pressing

Fading day overpowered by night

Melted Cheese

Have you noticed how the full moon
appears like a rich orange lantern
hanging low in the sky
changing lighter and brighter
as it climbs and arcs over
the sleeping world below?

As it wanes it seems to struggle –
tired perhaps of all that glory

And as our backs bend as we get older
so the perfect round seems to melt
in the top segment
like cheese under the grill
running out of sight down the side
of the toast

Between Heaven and Earth

Walking along the wintry beach
gloomy thoughts were utterly dispelled
by a perfectly arcing rainbow
suspended between heaven and earth
reflected briefly in the wet sand

But my attention was caught again
by the sight of two swans flying past
as if under the rainbow
their wings beating rhythmically
with such power and grace

Paddling in the turbulent waters
I watched warily the approaching mist
and gasped as it turned into rain
coming down sideways
soaking me to the skin in minutes

Shakespeare wrote in *Hamlet*
'There are more things in heaven and earth, Horatio…'
I don't think he was referring
to sights such as these
but I like his turn of phrase

Layer Upon Layer

Even with the clouds blocking the sun
reducing the ocean to a mass of
heaving grey and white
the striations on the cliff face
were vivid in their shades of red and brown
and with that wavy look
they reminded me of an unsuccessful attempt
at baking a layer cake

I'm not sure the green icing on top
had done much in the way of camouflage!

Mariners

I sat on my jacket on a rock
the sun gently warm on my back

Water in the marina still as glass
as father and small son
loaded gear on to their boat

No fancy yacht for them –
a small clinker-built craft
painted pea-green
with a folded sail
that looked for a moment
like a leaping lion

Life jacket safely on
the little boy held the tiller
as Dad untied the mooring ropes
and they reversed out   turned
and headed for the open sea

In the quiet
the boy's voice rang out
'Dad…'

The deeper voice responded
'Not yet…'

There was an ocean of affection
in their exchange

Comforting Sounds

There is much comfort to be had
late on a winter's afternoon
to hear the sounds of someone
in the kitchen
preparing a meal for me to share

When I was a child it was my mother
now it is Stephen busily paring raw vegetables
with that unmistakable rasp
of the potato peeler
accompanied by the clatter
of the chopping board
as it slips on the bench top
and used cutlery being tossed
into the sink
for me to wash later

Outside all is grey and overcast
and I am glad the lights are on

The smell of raw onions
makes my mouth water

I glance in anticipation at the clock…

Clean Sweep

There is nothing quite as invigorating
as a clean cold wind
sweeping unhindered along the beach

Dry sand swept before it
hissing a song of freedom won

Add a clear blue sky
early morning winter sun
the sound of waves
crashing to the shore –
the smell of the ocean

Who could resist the seduction
of running barefoot into the sea
feeling the swirl and pressure
around unsteady legs
as laughter bubbles up?

All Wrapped Up

I reached out to pluck
what I thought was a dead leaf
from the bougainvillea
but I was wrong

It had become an incubator

Small dead leaves from the tree above
were like blankets around a cocoon
all held in place
by fragile gossamer threads

Moving

The Earth is spinning and turning towards the east

We don't feel it move
rather measure in terms of the sun and the moon
travelling across the sky

I watched the sun lower below the horizon
my heart welling up with wonder
as the mystery of twilight unfolded

No clouds to gather colour to themselves
the clear sky holds it all

Rose-tinted apricot and lemon –
a halo of brightness
a flare of defiant radiance
cooling down and becoming ice blue
before the advancing blanket of night

A small pale sickle moon
kept Jupiter company

Much later I looked out
and the moon now lying on her back
almost out of sight
had turned mellow gold

Big Breakfast

Have you ever wondered
what the seagulls find
when they paddle their feet up and down
at the waterline
then thrust their beaks into the soft wet sand?

The youthful Pacific gull
already much larger than the silver gulls
answered that question this morning
when he revealed a very long pink worm
dangling from his beak

But earlier I had seen him
chasing a silver gull over the water
in a brilliant display of precision flight
and I find I am doubting
that he did the actual retrieving

Maybe he was just a bully-boy
taking the worm after all the work had been done
and I don't think I would have argued
if he came after me
wanting to take my big breakfast

Ah Well

Where did that beautiful clear morning go?

Where the little white-capped waves
sparkling along the tidal reach?

Gone is the pristine blue sky
the sheen of sunlight on dancing leaves

The wind is mournful at the door
rain spatters against the window
everything seems shrouded in greyness

Ah well, that's winter for you
tricking me into anticipation
of early spring

Endless Questions

I needed a break from endless questions
racing through my mind as I keep getting lost
in my studies of the ancient Greeks

So as a creature of habit
I headed out on the bike down to the beach
where I paddled my feet in the very cold water
and let the still silence seep in

I couldn't help but chuckle at the
worm trails like question marks in the sand
because it set me off
on another line of questions…

Promises of Spring

A clear blue sky with a vapour trail
that looks like an ellipsis on a page

Hardly a ripple on the tidal reach
except the little wash behind
each silver gull as they float like origami birds

The cormorants and grebes keep disappearing
under the surface

The sun is warm on my face
and I can smell the pungent herb of grace
on my fingers

I love pottering in the garden
on days like this
seeing new growth among the old
pulling out weeds
like the wrong words in a poem

Pastoral

A typical pastoral scene
with gently sloping green paddock
and oval-shaped dam
reflecting a pale blue sky

A giant dead gum tree –
half in half out of the water –
shone silver in the sunlight

Two or three black and white cows –
still as statues –
stood on the bank

Two more equally still
stood in the water itself

Transcending time and country
it could have been anywhere

Bush Walk

Out in the bush
grasses beside the narrow winding path
gleamed with sunlight
silver spears among the green

Tiny blue and mauve flowers (my favourites)
topped slender bending stems

Invisible insects buzzed –
birds called to each other
as if commentating on our progress

The steepness of the path
made us puff and
while not a hot day
we felt warm walking back from the lookout
where the river ran
through the gorge far below –
hard to see among the green of the trees

An echidna snuffled as it buried its head
in the dirt
convinced he could not be seen

His quills were magnificent
lying flat along his back

Denial

In a very neat front garden
is a narrow flower border
with large pebbles around the feet
of mounds of colourful flowers

Nestled between two mounds
a plover sits on her nest

Each time we have passed
she has been facing a different way
– but never towards the road

Garden Drama

The mother blackbird is anxiously
sitting on the gutter of the garden shed

Her fledgling offspring is among the weeds
near the low window
desperately raising itself up
as if seeking reassurance from its reflection

I glanced away and lost sight of it

Mum has swooped down
She is clucking around
not happy with me watching
as she goes into the weeds
to feed her baby

I want to watch this unfolding drama
yet don't want Mum to panic
and desert the little one

I will turn my back and watch the cows
in the water meadow
or write a poem about Miss Gracious
the beautiful grey and very large hen
who is scratching her way
around her domain
treating me with disdain

It's Still Out There

I glibly say,
'There are two pelicans on the posts this morning'
but nothing is ever that simple

What posts?
The ones that stand like sentinels –
relics of a bygone age –
where one pelican stretches its long neck
up   out   then down
to settle a stray feather

Then there are the silver gulls
gossiping and squawking   galahs are chattering
in the Norfolk Island pines   a pair of swallows
keep darting past
no doubt hunting for breakfast

The plovers are in competition
with the magpies carolling melodiously

Cars rumble over the road bridge   a train
trundles over the trellis bridge   a plane
is passing overhead

There are blipping sounds from the water –
some hidden creature coming up for air

I say it is *still* out there
but there is so much happening…

Red Wattlebird

We have called him Hitler
but that is unkind

He is simply a parent bird
wanting the breadcrumbs
for his hungry babies

No wonder he dive-bombs
the other birds
and snaps his wings
with a loud 'crack'

It is the way of nature

Petunias and Pansies

Petunias are like flamboyant frilly petticoats –
their sweet perfume released by the sun's warmth

Pansies with their friendly faces
don't seem to mind the winter chill
and stop the garden being too formal

Together they are vibrant splashes of yellow
pink   purple   white   mauve

Colours to warm the heart and soul
and raise a smile

Patience

New cherry tomatoes
dark red not scarlet

I'm not sure if I like the look of them
but the taste will be the test

Cucumbers grow fat so quickly
once the golden flowers set

We have two now
a few more days and they will be ready

Gardening teaches me patience
but I want it NOW

Crow's Nest

All summer I have watched
the new growth in the top of the
Norfolk Island pine and
although part of the main trunk
it is still only green latticework
and therefore very supple

A small parliament of crows
comes for lunch most days
learning how to swoop for bread
just like the silver gulls

The proud young tree trunk
has become the favoured perch
of one of the crows
and bends graciously under its weight –
though now it is unable to straighten up
when the bird leaves

Meanwhile the bird gazes around
as if atop a tall sailing mast
but I don't suppose his loud 'craak'
is calling 'Land ahoy'

Fairies at Work

There are those who say
they don't believe in fairies

Perhaps they have never ambled
around a garden
when the dew is still on leaves
and petals   curled and exotic
looking as if they are freshly painted
with tiny strokes of a lovingly held brush

Such aching loveliness
beyond words
almost beyond comprehension…

Hot Stuff

A galah was hanging upside down
by his beak from the power lines
perhaps to impress

Then he huddled close to his mate
whispering sweet nothings in her ear

If he had pecked too hard
I guess he would have really been
hot stuff

Flower Power

When snuggled up in bed
mind busy with things I cannot change
things keeping at bay healing sleep
I turn my thoughts and a smile comes
as I go slowly through the alphabet
naming flowers for each letter

I find myself walking again
all the gardens I have known –
the woods   orchards   meadows…
the Flower Fairy books
of my childhood
the Language of Flowers books
in my own library

What riches I have
at the fingertips of memory
to be shared joyfully
with those walking a darkened path

Slowing Heart and Mind

Here in the walled garden
the winter sun is warm on my face

It casts rainbows in the strands of my hair
as they dance in a soft cold breeze

Wind chimes vie with the chirping sparrows
for my attention

'What is this life if full of care
we have no time to stand and stare…'
How I love these lines from the poem
'Leisure'

How I love to sit somewhere
and let my heart and mind slow until
I can feel the blood flowing in my veins
knowing that in a life
rich and full with experiences
I will always be loved as I have loved
and I will forever walk
in a field of flowers

www.ingramcontent.com/pod-product-compliance
Lightning Source LLC
Chambersburg PA
CBHW062201100526
44589CB00014B/1903